Alpine Tundra
Life on the Tallest Mountain

Alpine Tundra
Life on the Tallest Mountain

Salvatore Tocci

Watts LIBRARY™

Franklin Watts
A Division of Scholastic Inc.
New York • Toronto • London • Auckland • Sydney
Mexico City • New Delhi • Hong Kong
Danbury, Connecticut

For my daughter Chris

Note to readers: Definitions for words in **bold** can be found in the Glossary at the back of this book.

Photographs © 2005: Corbis Images: 53 (Alissa Crandall), 32 (David Muench), 50 (Gianni Dagli Orti); Corbis Sygma/Viennareport Agency: 8; Dembinsky Photo Assoc.: 44 (Darrell Gulin), 6, 7 (Helen Olmsted); Peter Arnold Inc.: 28 (Doug Lee), 48, 49 (Jim Wark); Photo Researchers, NY: 40, 41 (Bill Bachman), 20 (Howard B. Bluestein), 43 (Kent & Donna Dannen), 5 right, 15 (Farrell Grehan), 35 (William J. Jahoda), 10 (Ken M. Johns), 37 (Adam Jones), 23 (G.C. Kelley), 30, 31 (Tom & Pat Leeson), 47 (C.K. Lorenz), 2 (Rafael Marcia), 29 (Maslowski), 22 (William H. Mullins), 17 (Stephen Saks), cover (Jim Steinberg), 38, 39 (Art Wolfe); Terry Donnelly: 5 left, 13, 18, 24, 54.

Map by XNR Productions

The photograph on the cover shows the French Alps. The photograph opposite the title page shows the view from the Karwendel Mountain Range in Germany.

Library of Congress Cataloging-in-Publication Data

Tocci, Salvatore.
    Alpine tundra / Salvatore Tocci.—1st ed.
       p. cm. — (Biomes and habitats)
    Includes bibliographical references (p.   ).
    ISBN 0-531-12365-0 (lib. bdg.)   0-531-16696-1 (pbk.)
    1. Tundra ecology—Juvenile literature. 2. Alpine regions—Juvenile literature. I. Title. II. Series.
QH541.5.T8T624 2005
577.5'86—dc22

                                     2004013583

Contents

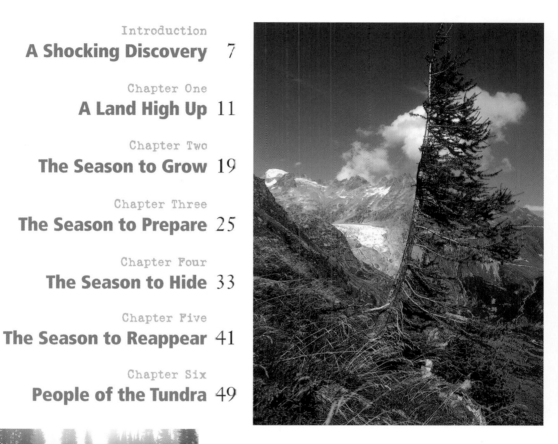

The Alps spread across Italy, Austria, Switzerland, Germany, France, and Slovenia.

A Shocking Discovery

On a September day in 1991, Helmut and Erika Simon were hiking through the Alps near the border between Austria and Italy. Although it was autumn, the ground high up in the mountains was covered with ice. Suddenly, the Simons came upon what they thought was a doll. As they approached to take a closer look, the Simons were shocked.

What looked like the head of a doll was actually the head and shoulders of a man. The rest of the man's body

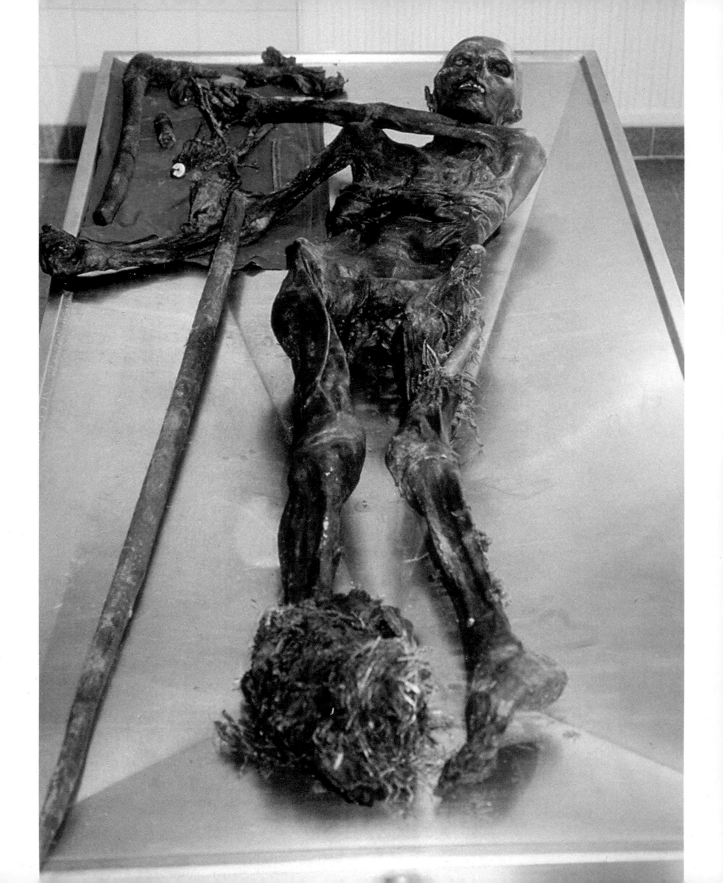

appeared to be frozen beneath the ice. The Simons quickly descended the mountain to report what they had found. Several people were sent to investigate. They immediately started working to free the body from the ice. They hacked away at the ice with axes, ski poles, and even a jackhammer. After four days, they finally succeeded in recovering the body. Like the Simons, everyone was amazed by what they saw.

The ice preserved even the clothing the man was wearing. His clothes were made from animal skins, and his boots were stuffed with grass to keep his feet warm. He had a beard, and his hair was long, dark, and wavy. He was carrying a stone knife and a copper ax.

Scientists later discovered that the man lived about five thousand years ago, during a time known as the Copper-Stone Age, or Early Bronze Age. They also learned that he had died at the spot where his body became covered with snow that slowly turned to ice. The man soon became known as the Iceman. The place where the Simons discovered the Iceman is the highest point at which any prehistoric human has been found in Europe.

An arrowhead discovered in the Iceman's left shoulder is believed to be the cause of his death.

*The alpine tundra
is similar to the
arctic, with cold
temperatures and
howling winds.*

Chapter One

A Land High Up

The region of the Alps in which the Iceman was discovered is known as the **alpine tundra**. The alpine tundra is one of several **biomes** on Earth. A biome is a geographic area whose environmental conditions determine the kinds of plants and animals that can live in it. The name "alpine tundra" is a clue as to what this biome is like. *Alpine* comes from the word *Alps*, the European mountain range in which the Iceman was discovered. *Tundra* may come from a Russian word that means "land of no trees." *Tundra* may also come from a Finnish word that means "barren hill." Therefore, the alpine tundra is a biome that exists high in the mountains where environmental conditions prevent trees and most everything else from growing.

Alpine tundra can be found on mountains in all parts of the world. For example, alpine tundra exists on the Rocky Mountains of North America, the Andes of South America, the Alps of Europe, the Himalayas of Asia, and the Snowy Mountains of Australia.

Where It Begins and Ends

The alpine tundra begins at the elevation where trees no longer grow on a mountain. This spot marks the **timberline**, which is the highest elevation at which trees grow. From the timberline, the alpine tundra extends upward toward the mountain peaks. The alpine tundra ends either at the top of the mountain or at the point where the ground is permanently covered with snow.

The elevation at which the alpine tundra starts on a mountain varies from place to place and depends on the regional climate. For example, the timberline in the southern Rockies is found between 11,500 and 12,000 feet (3,500 and 3,650 meters). The alpine tundra there starts at this elevation. Farther north, where the weather is colder and wetter, the timberline drops to 9,500 feet (2,900 m) in Wyoming and then to 7,500 feet (2,300 m) in Montana. In these places, the alpine

Way Up North

A different tundra biome, known as the arctic tundra, exists in the far northern latitudes.

No Trees

In northern Alaska, trees do not grow on mountains, even at sea level.

Alpine tundra is found above the timberline on a mountain.

tundra begins on the mountain at these lower elevations, where trees can grow in the milder climate.

Getting to the Alpine Tundra

The alpine tundra is the only biome that you have to climb a mountain to reach. Before reaching the alpine tundra, you will probably pass through several other biomes. For example, imagine that your journey begins at a spot in the western United States. As you look around, you see nothing but flat ground covered with sand. The only living things you see are cactus plants and brush. The climate is hot and dry. You are in a biome known as a desert.

Your next stop takes you to a place where it is cooler and perhaps even raining. As you look around, you see mostly tall grasses. Animals, such as bison, are grazing. You are now in a biome called a grassland, which is more commonly known in North America as a prairie.

As you continue your journey, you next reach a forest where the trees are beginning to lose their leaves. This biome is called a temperate deciduous forest. Your journey next takes

Antarctica is the only place on Earth without a biome.

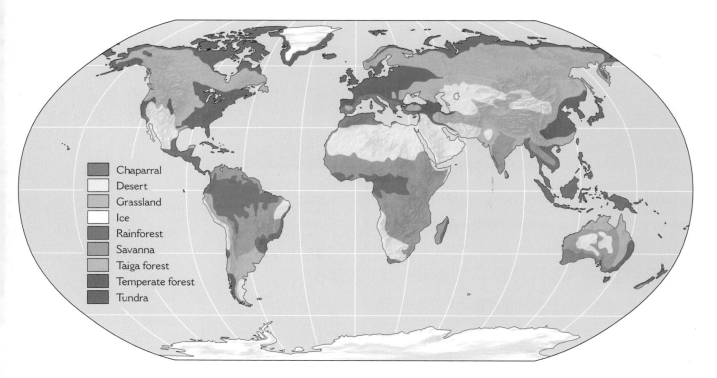

Chaparral
Desert
Grassland
Ice
Rainforest
Savanna
Taiga forest
Temperate forest
Tundra

you to a forest where only evergreen trees, such as pines and firs, can be seen. You have reached a biome called a **taiga**, which stretches to the base of a mountain. As you climb the mountain, you continue to pass through evergreen trees. You notice that the trees gradually thin out as you continue to climb.

Suddenly, you emerge from the evergreen forest. The trees you now see are strange looking. They are short, with trunks and branches that are twisted into strange shapes. These trees are called krummholz, which comes from the German words for "crooked wood." Growing high on the mountain, they are bent by the strong winds that are common at this elevation. With their shiny trunks, these trees look more dead than alive. As you continue to climb the mountain, the trees become even more twisted and stunted. Suddenly, you do not see any trees. You have reached your destination. You are now in the alpine tundra.

A krummholz tree can live for more than 1,500 years.

A Barren Place

More Air

At 14,000 feet (4,300 m), a person needs to breathe almost twice as much air to get the same amount of oxygen as is available at sea level.

Looking at the alpine tundra for the first time, a person is likely to agree that the Finnish word *tundra*, meaning "barren hill," is an appropriate name for this biome. The ground is rocky. Small boulders are scattered across the land, which seems lifeless. Only a few animals, if any, can be seen. Plants that grow here are tiny and can easily be overlooked.

Breathing the air at this elevation can be difficult. Not only is the air cold, it also contains less oxygen than does air at ground level. Faster and deeper breaths are necessary to get enough oxygen. A person visiting the alpine tundra may develop acute mountain sickness from the lack of oxygen. Symptoms of acute mountain sickness include headache, dizziness, and nausea.

During the day, the sun highlights the starkness of the alpine tundra. The lack of trees or anything tall means that there are no long shadows to create contrasts with the bright whiteness of the snow. The air is crystal clear, with fewer dust and haze particles to block the sun's rays. As a result, there can

A Wise Saying

A person exploring the alpine tundra should wear lotion or cream to block the sun's rays. Twice as many of the sun's damaging ultraviolet rays reach this elevation on the mountain than reach ground level. Over time, exposure to the sun in the alpine tundra can damage the skin and cause cancer. People who live in the alpine tundra in the Andes of South America have a saying: "Only foreigners and donkeys walk in the sunshine."

be 25 percent more sunlight in the alpine tundra than there is at sea level. People visiting this region must always wear sunglasses to protect their eyes from the sun. Although it seems that there is little life here, the alpine tundra is a place where life exists throughout all four seasons of the year.

Without sunglasses or goggles, a person may become snow-blind in the alpine tundra.

Plants are in full bloom in the alpine tundra, where the growing, or frost-free, season in summer may be as short as thirty days.

Chapter Two

The Season to Grow

The summer is the time of year when life, both plant and animal, is most visible on the alpine tundra. Even in summer, however, snow covers the ground in many places. The temperature can be 30 degrees cooler than it is at the base of the mountain. While it may be raining at the base, the colder temperature causes snow to fall on the alpine tundra. A summer storm can produce several feet of snow.

In the alpine tundra of the Rockies, July is the warmest month. During the day, the temperature rarely drops below freezing, and it may get as high as 60 degrees Fahrenheit (15 degrees Celsius). The average daily temperature is in the forties. Nights, however, are almost always below freezing.

Unpredictable Weather

One summer day in the alpine tundra may be cool, dry, and very windy. Another summer day may be warmer, wetter, and calmer. Even the dry, warmer days are almost always interrupted by brief but intense thunderstorms. These storms occur nearly every day in summer. Most thunderstorms only last for half an hour or less. The water from the rain, combined with the water from the melting snow, saturates the ground. Plants that thrive in the tundra's short growing season use this water.

Thunderstorms bring most of the water to the alpine tundra in summer.

Small and Hardy

The alpine tundra is one of the harshest environments that any **organism**, or living thing, faces. The cold temperatures, strong winds, and exposed landscape make survival a challenge that must be overcome almost every day, even in the summer. Every organism must have the **adaptations** to survive the harsh conditions of the tundra. An adaptation is a feature that increases an organism's chances of survival.

One adaptation that alpine tundra plants share is their small size, with stems that usually grow no more than 10 inches (25 centimeters) high. Their short height keeps them close to the ground, where they are not as exposed to high winds. Hugging the ground also provides them with warmth coming from the soil that has been heated by the summer sun.

Some of the plants that hug the ground are known as cushion plants. These plants look like dome-shaped cushions made of tiny green leaves and colorful blossoms. Although their stems, leaves, and flowers rise only a short distance above the ground, their roots can extend as much as 6 feet (2 m) into the ground. This deep root system anchors them to the ground and enables them to absorb as much water as possible. As summer arrives in the tundra, cushion plants are the first to produce blossoms of many colors, including blues, pinks, yellows, and reds.

The colors that appear on cushion plants lure bees and butterflies from their hiding places. These animals are among the first to emerge from the ground, where they have kept warm

Watermelon Snow

Where snow does cover the ground in summer, it may have a reddish color and is therefore known as watermelon snow. The reddish color of this snow is caused by tiny organisms called algae. Each of these organisms is surrounded by a reddish, jellylike coat that protects it from the sun's rays. These algae collect in large numbers as the snow begins to melt in summer. One teaspoon (5 milliliters) of melting snow may contain as many as 500,000 algae.

The leaves of this colorful cushion plant are covered with tiny hairs that block wind and trap heat.

while awaiting the arrival of summer. These insects immediately begin to fly among the plants, sipping nectar from the colorful blossoms. Some of the butterflies and bees have formed a close relationship with a particular kind of plant. The parnassian butterfly is an example. While it is developing into its adult form, this butterfly feeds almost exclusively on the yellow stonecrop plant. This plant produces a poison that discourages all animals except the parnassian butterfly from feeding on it. The poison, in turn, discourages birds from feeding on the butterfly.

Mostly Perennials

Almost all alpine tundra plants are **perennials**. A perennial plant is one that lives for more than two growing seasons. The perennials that grow in summer on the tundra are mainly grasses and sedges. Sedges look like grasses, but they have solid rather than hollow stems.

With such a short growing season, tundra plants must reach their full size quickly. This is usually not much of a problem, because even the grasses and sedges do not grow very tall. An example is a sedge called *Kobresia*, which gets no taller than a person's hand. This plant grows quickly but only in places that are free of snow, even in winter. *Kobresia* may cover more than half of the ground in such places. Its widespread growth is the result of its ability to soak up water from the ground much faster than other plants can. Its ability to grow so well and so fast has enabled some *Kobresia* plants to live for more than two hundred years.

Like the cushion plants, *Kobresia* plants also attract animals, but in this case much larger ones. Populations of elk, deer, and mountain sheep graze on this sedge plant. Like most tundra grasses and sedges, the *Kobresia* plant has a high **nutrient** content. A nutrient is a substance that an organism needs to survive and grow. Animals must get the nutrients they will need to survive the coming seasons.

Grasses and sedges make up 85 percent of an elk's diet in the summer.

The fall colors in the alpine tundra can be more brilliant than the fall foliage in a forest.

Chapter Three

The Season to Prepare

Fall can be the driest season in the alpine tundra. Summer thunderstorms no longer bring rain. At the start of the season, snowfalls are rare events. In fact, during September and October, a warm fall is not unusual. Daytime temperatures may be 40 degrees warmer than they are at night. Early fall is the time for organisms to start preparing for winter. By late October, the average daily temperature is below freezing. Starting in November, half the days may be snowy.

In late fall, ice begins to form on ponds and streams. Just below the ground, water freezes to form long needles of ice that point toward the surface. These ice needles slowly get longer and eventually poke through the surface, where they look like icicles sticking up from the ground. As ice needles emerge from the ground, they uproot the soil. In doing so, they tear apart the roots of plants. Perennials whose roots are damaged may not return in the next growing season.

A Change of Colors

As the temperature changes, so do the colors displayed by tundra plants. The bright yellows, blues, reds, and pinks of summer start to disappear as flowers wither, leaving only the green of the leaves and stems. As the temperature continues to drop, even the green begins to fade.

As the green fades from the tundra, the colors of fall start to emerge. Cushion plants, grasses, and sedges begin to display the shades of fall: red, orange, yellow, bronze, brown, and gold. These plants display a wider range of colors than do those that grow at lower elevations on the mountain. In addition, the fall colors in the alpine tundra form a striking contrast with the stark white snow and the bright blue sky.

The shorter, colder days of fall are a signal to plants to stop growing. Nutrients made by the leaves and stems during the summer are transported and stored in the roots. Most leaves cannot withstand the freezing temperatures and will die and fall from the plant. The frost preserves the dead leaves, so they will not decompose until the spring. As a result, fewer nutrients will be returned to the soil. This is one reason the soil in the alpine tundra cannot grow a more diverse group of plants.

Plant Adaptations

Tundra plants have various adaptations to help them meet the challenges presented by the cooler fall temperatures. One example of an adaptation can be seen in the paintbrush plant. Like many tundra plants, the paintbrush has red-tinged leaves. The red color is due to a pigment called **anthocyanin**. This red pigment is present in the leaves of most plants, but it is usually overshadowed by the green pigment **chlorophyll**. As temperatures get cooler in fall, the chlorophyll begins to break down, revealing the anthocyanins with their red color.

A Rocky Soil

In addition to being nutrient poor, the soil in the alpine tundra is thin and rocky. Constant winds blow away finer soil particles, preventing them from collecting and forming a thicker layer of soil. The rocks found in the soil today were deposited by glaciers thousands of years ago. Today, about half the ground in some places is covered with small rocks. Such places are called fellfields. The rest is covered with soil.

The rocks that litter a fellfield were once underground. As water in the ground froze, the rocks were forced upward. As the ground thawed, the rocks again retreated into the ground. Over many years, the repeated cycle of freezing and thawing arranged the rocks so that they formed patterns on the surface. One such pattern is a polygon in which the rocks form a structure that encloses a small area of tundra soil.

In addition to red, paintbrush plants also produce pink, pale yellow, and rose flowers.

Anthocyanins can convert light energy from the sun into heat, which helps keep tundra plants warm in the fall.

Tundra plants adapt in other ways when temperatures fall below freezing. Most leaves and stems cannot withstand freezing temperatures and begin to die. As they fall to the ground, they form a protective cover over the remaining plant parts that will remain inactive until the next growing season. Many plants also begin to produce hardened scales to cover fragile parts that would otherwise die because of the frost.

Animal Adaptations

Unlike the plants, many tundra animals can leave the biome as the fall season progresses. Most birds migrate to warmer areas because they cannot survive the freezing temperatures and lack of food. Such birds include flickers, bluebirds, larks, finches, and sparrows. Most birds travel only a short distance, moving down the mountain where they will remain until spring returns to the alpine tundra. Others, such as the American pipit that lives in the tundra of the Rocky Mountains, fly as far south as Mexico.

Only one bird has the adaptations needed to remain a year-round resident of the Rocky Mountain tundra. This is the white-tailed ptarmigan. In autumn, this bird grows a coat of down feathers to help insulate itself against the cold weather. The feathers, which are especially thick along its back, also trap air that adds to the insulation. As winter approaches, these feathers change color from brown to white. These white

The white feathers serve not only as insulation but also as camouflage to protect the ptarmigan from being eaten.

Feathers All Over

The ptarmigan's legs and feet are also covered with feathers, unlike those of most birds.

feathers help protect the bird by camouflaging it against the snow. Short feathers even line the ptarmigan's nostrils to warm the air it breathes before the air reaches the bird's lungs.

Other animals that will remain in the tundra during the winter spend the autumn preparing. Pikas, which are closely related to rabbits, gather as much vegetation as possible. They store the food in underground dens, where they will spend the winter. Their short legs, small ears, and lack of a tail will help them conserve heat. A growth of dense fur and a buildup of fat inside their bodies will also help keep them warm. Other small tundra animals will also develop thicker fur coats and store body fat during the fall. These include marmots and ground squirrels.

As winter approaches, the dwindling supply of food will force many of the large tundra animals to migrate down the mountain. These include deer, mountain lions, coyotes, and elk. For the most part, only bighorn sheep and mountain goats will remain. Male and female bighorn sheep remain in separate groups during most of the year. However, late fall is

their mating season. Of all the large tundra animals, mountain goats are best adapted to the cold weather. During the fall, their bodies will become covered with thick fur to protect them during the winter season.

Two male bighorn sheep battle during the fall mating season.

With respect to the temperature, climbing 1,000 feet (305 m) up Pikes Peak is the same as traveling 600 miles (960 km) north.

Chapter Four

The Season to Hide

Winters in the alpine tundra are brutal. The first weather station in the United States to study the alpine winter began operating in 1873 on the summit of Pikes Peak in Colorado. Information, including temperature, wind speed, and barometric pressure, was sent by telegraph to Colorado Springs. In winter, however, transmitting this information was not always possible. As much as 6 inches (15 cm) of ice would sometimes collect on the telegraph lines, causing them to

Fast Mover

An avalanche can travel as fast as 200 miles per hour (320 km per hour).

break. When information about the weather was sent, it became very clear why most tundra animals hide during the winter.

Snowfalls occur almost every day, resulting in large accumulations. During the winter of 1978–1979, nearly 70 feet (21 m) of snow covered some spots in the Rocky Mountain tundra. During the winter, temperatures never get above freezing. At night, they can drop to –40 degrees F (–40 degrees C). Fierce winds make it feel much colder. Even moderate winds still blow between 30 and 40 miles per hour (48 and 64 km per hour). Winter winds pick up, blow, and redeposit snow to form huge drifts. In some places, a snowdrift may extend past the edge of a mountain ridge. This snowdrift may fall from the edge and start an avalanche.

Surviving the Harsh Conditions

Snowdrifts may cause an avalanche, but they can also help tundra animals survive. For example, ptarmigans seek protection from the blowing wind and snow by positioning themselves in the hollow of a snowdrift. In fact, if it were not for the protection provided by snowdrifts, most ptarmigans would die from exposure. Besides forming snowdrifts, the wind helps these birds in another way. Winds uncover buds and twigs buried beneath the snow. By feeding on this vegetation, ptarmigans can actually gain weight during the winter.

Many small animals escape the winter weather by living in the layer between the snow cover and the ground. Animals that live in this layer include pikas, mice, shrews, gophers, and voles. The temperature in this layer is much warmer than the air temperature above the snow. These small animals spend much of the winter huddled in their nests. They venture outdoors only to search for vegetation to eat. However, they must be very careful whenever they leave the protection of their layer.

Gophers tunnels can be seen when the snow begins to melt.

Aboveground, larger animals, especially weasels and snowshoe hares, also search for food. Weasels thrive in the snow and remain outdoors during the winter. Their coat color changes from brown to white, camouflaging them against the snow. However, their coats do not get thicker with the colder weather and therefore do not provide them with any additional insulation. Weasels survive outdoors by consuming as many small animals as they can find. All this food fuels their high **metabolisms**. The metabolism of an animal represents all the processes needed to keep it alive. These processes include digestion and respiration. A high metabolism in winter provides the body warmth these animals need to survive.

The largest tundra animals that survive the winter include mountain goats, bighorn sheep, and any elks that did not migrate to lower elevations. These animals survive in part by having extra insulation from fur that grew thicker in the fall. They continuously move from place to place, searching for any vegetation not covered by snow.

Surviving Underground

Some tundra animals, such as marmots and ground squirrels, spend the entire winter in burrows they have dug underground. During this time, these animals enter **hibernation**, which is a time during which their bodies become inactive. A hibernating animal's body temperature drops to several degrees above the freezing point. Its heart beats so slowly that the beats are barely noticeable. It breathes only a few times a minute. In effect, any signs of life would be difficult to detect in an animal that is in hibernation.

Marmots are the largest **rodents** that live in the alpine tundra. Rodents have teeth that are specialized for gnawing. An adult rodent can weigh 10 pounds (5 kg) in late fall after eating as much as possible in preparation for winter. Marmots store the energy from this food in their bodies as fat.

Fat is high in energy, which can be measured in calories. Breaking down fat releases this energy, mostly in the form of heat. Brown fat contains even more calories than regular, or white, fat. While marmots hibernate, their bodies break down brown fat to supply enough heat to keep them warm. Marmots actually hibernate for most of the year, from September through April.

Marmots spend most of their lives hibernating in burrows, but they come out in late spring and summer to bask in the sun.

Strange Sound

The ground squirrel is called "tsik-tsik" by the Inuits because of the call it makes when alarmed.

Like marmots, ground squirrels almost double their body weight during the fall by eating as much as possible to prepare for hibernation. Unlike a marmot, however, a ground squirrel will periodically emerge from its hibernation, move around for a short time, and then begin hibernating again. As it enters hibernation, a ground squirrel's body temperature will get close to the freezing point. This is the lowest known body temperature of any living **mammal**, which is an animal that has hair and can regulate its body temperature.

Surrounded by Ice

All the animals discussed so far are able to regulate their body temperatures to help them survive the tundra winter. These animals are sometimes known as **warm-blooded** animals. Some tundra animals, however, are said to be **cold-blooded**, which means they cannot regulate their body temperatures. Cold-blooded animals that live on the alpine tundra include insects, toads, frogs, and fishes.

Most of these animals spend part or all of their lives in lakes, ponds, and streams whose surface water freezes in win-

ter. Some cold-blooded animals, such as frogs, bury themselves in the muddy bottoms and fall into a deep sleep. If the water is shallow enough, the entire pond or stream may freeze. In this case, the animals produce substances that act like antifreeze to protect themselves from the surrounding ice. Like all the other animals trying to survive the tundra winter, they are waiting for the next season.

Even in summer, the water temperature of a tundra pond may not get above 40 degrees F (4 degrees C).

39

Many expert skiers head to the alpine tundra in spring, when corn snow makes for perfect conditions.

Chapter Five

The Season to Reappear

In the Alps, Germans call it *sulzschnee*. In the Rocky Mountains, Americans call it corn snow. No matter what it's called, this is the snow that forms in the alpine tundra during the spring. Spring brings temperatures that rise above freezing during the day, only to fall back down during the night. The cycle of thawing and freezing causes the top layer of snow to melt and refreeze into tiny ice grains. During the day, these ice grains are loose. At night, however, they pack together.

41

Spring brings not only warmer temperature, but also longer days, fewer clouds, and less precipitation. By June, the average daily temperature remains above freezing. Now is the time for life to reappear on the alpine tundra.

Spring Flowers

Magenta primrose, sky blue forget-me-nots, golden parsley, and white candytuft are among the earliest spring bloomers. Many plants start to grow even before the snow melts completely. This is possible because these alpine plants can carry out **photosynthesis** at cooler temperatures than those that grow at lower elevations can. Photosynthesis is the process by which plants produce nutrients, such as sugars. In winter, these sugars had served as antifreeze to protect the dormant plants. In spring, these sugars take on a new role, providing the energy the tundra plants need to grow.

One flower that also makes its appearance at this time of year is appropriately called the alpine spring beauty. Like

Growing on Rocks

In addition to grasses, sedges, and short flowering plants, other types of vegetation that grow in an alpine tundra include mosses and lichens. Mosses and lichens grow on the ground and on rocks. Mosses are primitive plants that do not form true roots, stems, or leaves. Lichens, however, are not even plants. They are a combination of two different types of organisms, an alga and a fungus. The alga supplys nutrients, while the fungus provides shelter.

many tundra plants, it hugs the ground, growing to be only about 1 inch (2.5 cm) high. As a result, alpine spring beauty plants are often overlooked by visitors to the region. However, their clusters of white to deep pink flowers help to attract attention. Although they are short plants, alpine spring beauties develop roots that penetrate as deep as 6 feet (2 m) into the soil, allowing the plant to grow in rock crevices.

The root of the alpine spring beauty plant is as thick as a thumb and can be eaten.

Spring is the time for small animals, such as this ground squirrel, to reappear on the tundra.

Awakenings

Spring is the time for animals to come out of hibernation. They gradually raise their body temperature by using up their remaining brown fat. As their body temperatures rise, their heart and breathing rates also increase. Marmots emerge from their burrows in late April or early May by digging tunnels through the snow cover.

Ground squirrels emerge sooner, as early as March if the weather is warm enough. Males emerge about two weeks before females do. Food is still scarce because of the snow cover. As a result, ground squirrels feed on food they stock-piled before they began their winter hibernation.

With the coming of spring, animals that spent the winter in the layer between the snow cover and the ground often face more of a challenge than those that had been hibernating. Warmer temperatures melt the snow, causing water to seep beneath the snow cover. In some cases, the animals living there drown. Many of those that do survive get wet, which lowers their body temperatures. If their body temperatures drop too far, these animals may die from **hypothermia**, which is a condition that occurs when the body temperature gets very low. Those that survive flooding and hypothermia must venture out in search of food. When they do, they must be careful to avoid larger animals that are also searching for food. Pikas, for example, immediately run for cover under rocks when they hear the slightest noise.

Mating Season

Spring is also the time for many tundra animals to reproduce. Most of them must do so as early as possible so that their young have time to grow large enough before the next winter arrives. The gopher is one example. Gophers breed in April or May. Females then give birth three and a half weeks later to a litter of between three and ten gophers. Female marmots give birth to between three and eight young just four to five weeks after mating.

Ptarmigans that survived the winter aboveground start to **molt**, or produce a new covering of feathers. Starting in late April, a male ptarmigan develops feathers with dark patches on its head and neck. Although females start to molt later, they do so more quickly than males do. Eventually, both males and females develop their warm-weather colors, with black and yellow feathers on their backs and tan-colored ones on their bellies.

Usually, the same male and female ptarmigan form a mating pair every spring. The female builds a nest that she lines with feathers pulled from her body. She then lays one egg per

With the arrival of spring, a ptarmigan produces a new coat of feathers.

day for as many as eleven days. However, she will not sit on any of the eggs until they have all been laid. This way, all the eggs will hatch at the same time.

The first recorded climb by humans to the top of Pikes Peak took place in 1820.

Chapter Six

People of the Tundra

The beauty of the alpine tundra has attracted people for some time. When the weather permitted, prehistoric hunters pursued large animals, such as elk and bighorn sheep. In addition to being a source of food, the alpine tundra was also considered sacred by the people who once inhabited this biome in the Rocky Mountains.

American Indians

Many **artifacts**, or human-made objects, have been discovered in the alpine tundra of the Rocky Mountains. Some of these artifacts were made by American Indians who first inhabited the tundra 6,000 to 7,500 years ago. These artifacts range in size from small, sharpened spear points that were used to kill animals to large stone walls that were used to trap animals.

The American Indians built up these walls, incorporating such natural barriers as cliffs and lakes as part of their structures. Some walls extended for more than half a mile (800 m)

Before they had horses, the American Indians living in the tundra had to rely on stone walls to trap large animals for food.

and were built to form a U- or V-shaped pattern. Scientists think that as many as fifty people worked as a group during a hunt, which usually occurred in the fall. Some hunters would drive the animals toward the walls. Others waited, hiding behind the rocks. Once the animals were trapped inside the walls, the hunters emerged with weapons drawn.

Once their hunt was finished, the American Indians took the animals to a place near a source of water. There, they used stone knives and scrapers to prepare the meat. Some of the meat was roasted over campfires and eaten. Some was hung to dry so that it could be eaten in the winter. When winter did arrive, the American Indians left the alpine tundra and moved to warmer climates. Today, American Indians no longer call the tundra their home. However, humans still inhabit this mountain biome in other parts of the world.

Obtaining Food

While the American Indian men hunted, the women gathered and preserved tundra plants.

The Incas and Sherpas

Natives in Peru call the alpine tundra in the Andes Mountains their home. Their ancestors first started living there some 10,000 years ago. People known as sherpas call the tundra in the Himalaya Mountains in Napal their home. Their ancestors started living there between 20,000 and 25,000 years ago, long before any humans inhabited the alpine tundra in other parts of the world.

People who live in the alpine tundra are known as highlanders. Besides the extreme weather conditions, highlanders must also face the challenge of breathing air that contains less

Long-Term Effects

After living at high altitudes for many years, elderly high-landers can develop an illness that causes them to have trouble breathing, to get tired easily, and to have aches and pains.

oxygen than does the air at lower elevations. Lack of oxygen can lead to a condition called **hypoxia**, or altitude sickness, for anyone not used to living in the alpine tundra.

Hypoxia comes on slowly. First, a person feels light-headed. A headache usually develops, and breathing often becomes more difficult. A person may become dizzy, feel nau-seated, and finally fall into unconsciousness. Getting down from the mountain may be the only way to avoid death.

Highlanders have various adaptations to help them sur-vive at high altitudes. First, their lung capacity is larger than that of people living at lower elevations. This means high-landers can take in more air, and therefore more oxygen, with every breath. Second, highlanders have more red blood cells, which are responsible for transporting oxygen throughout the body. The more red blood cells they have, the more oxygen their blood can carry. Third, their **hemo-globin**, which is the substance in red blood cells that carries oxygen, is different from the hemoglobin found in people living at lower elevations. The hemoglobin in highlanders carries more oxygen.

Visitors

The alpine tundra has long attracted visitors for various rea-sons. Early explorers came for the challenge of reaching the high peaks of the Rocky Mountains. Among the first was Zebulon Pike, who attempted to climb one of the peaks of the Rockies in 1806. This mountain top is now called Pikes Peak,

Prison Workers

A main road to the Rocky Mountain tun-dra was built during the early 1900s by prisoners from the Colorado State Peni-tentiary.

52

after this first recorded visitor. Zebulon Pike, however, never made it to the top.

In the 1820s, scientists arrived in the region and began collecting plant specimens. They sold much of what they collected to museums in order to raise funds for future visits to the tundra. In the 1850s, gold was discovered on Pikes Peak. Miners soon flocked to the tundra in search of their fortunes. In the 1880s, railroads were built to bring even more visitors to the tundra. Roads followed in the early 1900s. In the 1930s, the first ski resorts opened.

Today, tens of thousands of hikers, campers, skiers, and drivers visit the alpine tundra, mainly to appreciate its beauty. Unfortunately, their visits have come with a price. In summer, visitors are often unaware of the vegetation blooming underfoot and accidentally trample the tiny plants. To see the unique fall colors, visitors create their own walking paths and crush much of the vegetation that is preparing for winter.

Mines in the Rocky Mountain alpine tundra once contained gold, silver, gems, and valuable minerals.

Although its name means "land of no trees," the alpine tundra is a land in which life exists despite the harsh climate.

In winter, snowmobiles compress the snow. As a result, the layer beneath the snow cover may be 10 degrees colder than in areas where the snow has not been compacted. Animals hiding from winter weather conditions may not be able to survive these colder temperatures. In spring, litter left by humans may cover dormant plants and prevent them from growing.

Fortunately, more people are now aware of the variety of life that exists on the alpine tundra. They recognize that every effort must be made to protect this biome where life is so fragile because of the harsh conditions that exist year-round.

Glossary

adaptation—feature that increases an organism's chances of survival

alpine tundra—biome located on a mountain between the timberline and the permanent snow cover

anthocyanin—red pigment found in plants

artifact—human-made object, such as a tool

biome—geographic area with certain environmental conditions where specific kinds of plants and animals live

chlorophyll—green pigment found in plants

cold-blooded—not having the ability to regulate body temperature

hemoglobin—substance in red blood cells that transports oxygen

hibernation—extended period of time, usually in winter, in which many body processes, such as breathing, slow down

hypothermia—condition caused by unusually low body temperature

hypoxia—condition caused by the lack of oxygen at high altitudes

mammal—animal with hair or fur, the ability to regulate its body temperature, and the ability to produce milk if female

metabolism—processes that occur in the body, such as digestion, that are necessary for survival

molt—to replace the body covering, such as feathers or the skin, with new growth

nutrient—substance that an organism needs to survive and grow

organism—living thing

perennial—plant that lives for at least two years

photosynthesis—process by which plants make sugars and other nutrients

rodent—animal, such as a rat or mouse, that has teeth specialized for gnawing

taiga—biome south of the arctic tundra in which forests of evergreen trees are common

timberline—elevation that marks the highest point at which trees grow

warm-blooded—having the ability to regulate body temperature

To Find Out More

Books

Gellhorn, Joyce. *Song of the Alpine*. Johnson Books, 2002.

Harris, Tim. *Mountains and Highlands* (Biomes Atlases). Raintree/Steck Vaugh, 2003.

Sayre, April Pulley. *Tundra* (Exploring Earth's Biomes). 21st Century Books, 1997.

Organizations and Online Sites

Rocky Mountain National Park
http://www.nps.gov/romo/resources/plantsandanimals/ecosystem/alpinetundra.html
Get a list of many plants and animals that live in the alpine

tundra of the Rocky Mountains. Click on "Weekly Tidbit" to learn more details about a tundra plant or animal. You can also search this site for past tidbits by date or topic.

Alpine
http://www.blueplanetbiomes.org/alpine.htm
This site contains more information about the organisms and climate of the alpine tundra, including those of the Himalaya and Andes Mountains.

Pikes Peak Cam
http://www.pikespeakcam.com/
You can view live pictures taken by a video camera that operates on Pikes Peak twenty-four hours a day. Weather information is also updated every five minutes.

The Alpine Tundra
http://www.uwsp.edu/geo/projects/virtdept/ipvjft/tundra.html
See a photograph of a polygon formed by the cycle of freezing and thawing of the tundra soil. Also read about how the nature of the alpine tundra has changed as a result of natural causes and human activities.

The Sherpas
http://www.tengboche.com/trekking/ecology.htm
Read more about the sherpas and their role in mountain-climbing expeditions, including the first expedition to reach the top of Everest in 1953.

A Note on Sources

Two books that focus on the Rocky Mountain alpine tundra provided background information. *Land Above the Trees* by Ann H. Zwinger offers comprehensive coverage of the plants that live in this biome. *Song of the Alpine* by Joyce Gellhorn has more coverage of the animals and how they adapt to the changing seasons.

As always, the next step was to search the Internet for additional information. Finding out about the alpine tundra outside the Rocky Mountains was especially difficult, as very little information is available. Most of what is posted deals with the highlanders and their adaptations to high-altitude living. When searching the Internet, only sources that can be considered reliable were examined. These included sites run by government agencies, wildlife organizations, and educational institutions.

—Salvatore Tocci

Index

Numbers in *italics* indicate illustrations.

About the Author

Salvatore Tocci taught high school and college science for almost thirty years. He has a bachelor's degree from Cornell University and a Master of Philosophy degree from The City University of New York.

He has written books that deal with a range of science topics, from biographies about famous scientists to a high school chemistry textbook. He has also traveled throughout the United States to present workshops at national science conventions to show teachers how to emphasize the applications of scientific knowledge to students in their everyday lives.

Tocci lives in East Hampton, New York, with his wife Patti. They have skied several times in Colorado, where they were impressed by the beauty of the Rocky Mountains and its alpine tundra.